Gluten-Free Crock Pot Recipes

50 Sensational Set & Forget Slow Cooker Recipes for a Gluten-Free Diet

By

Mike Moreland

ISBN: 1508578931

ISBN-13: 978-1508578932

Table of Contents

Table of Contents

Table of Contents

Introduction

If you're gluten intolerant like me, you know how difficult it can be to keep to your diet with all the gluten containing products out there. You always have to be careful of what you eat, study the label of every packaged food item you buy, and cooking or eating out can be a challenge sometimes. So personally, I welcome anything that makes my gluten-free diet a little easier. And the crock pot does just that!

When I first started using a crock pot a few years ago, I wished I had discovered it sooner. The restrictions of a gluten-free diet are enough of a hassle for me and I don't particularly enjoy spending lots of time in the kitchen to prepare meals. With a crock pot, cooking becomes a whole lot easier, faster and more convenient.

Because this is a cookbook, we won't go into the specifics of living a gluten-free lifestyle, how to successfully stick to your diet, knowing what foods you can and cannot eat etc. If you'd like to know more about this, please check out my book *Gluten-Free Made Easy: The Complete Guide to Jump-Start Your Gluten-Free Diet.*[1]

---

[1] For an overview of my books: www.amazon.com/author/mikemoreland.

Introduction

Benefits of a Crock Pot

The most important benefits of using a crock pot are:

- **Set and forget**. For many recipes, you can just toss all the ingredients in the crock pot, let it do its magic, and a few hours later you can enjoy a delicious meal. No need to spend a lot of time in front of a hot stove. While the crock pot is preparing your meal, you have time to do other things. It doesn't get any better than that!

- **Meals are more nutritious and have better flavor**. Valuable nutrients are better preserved when foods are cooked for a longer time. Slow cooking also gives better intensity and distribution of flavors.

- **More convenience**. Nobody is excited to start cooking after a long working day. Let your crock pot do its thing while you are at work, so you can come home to a delicious hot meal. Or, let the crock pot cook overnight so your breakfast is ready when you wake up.

- **Clean-up is fast and easy**. Because everything is cooked in one dish, there's less to clean up after a meal. And if you use a removable liner for your crock pot, clean-up will be even faster and easier.

Crock Pots and Slow Cookers

"Crock-Pot" is a registered trade name of a slow cooker made by the company "Rival". This cooker became very popular and over time "crock pot" became a generic term that was used to refer to any type of slow cooker.

The terms crock pot and slow cooker are commonly used interchangeably. But whereas most people see them as referring to exactly the same thing, there are, in fact, some differences between a crock pot and a slow cooker. Basically, **every crock pot is a slow cooker, but not every slow cooker is a crock pot**. This sounds confusing, so allow me to explain this.

A crock pot has heating elements on both the bottom and the sides of the pot. It usually has only two main cook settings: "low" and "high". Other types of slow cookers, on the other hand, have their heating elements on the bottom of the cooker, not on the sides. They also have different cook settings, usually numbered from one to five. So in essence, a crock pot is a specific (and popular) type of slow cooker.

Crock Pot Tips

Before we get to the recipes, here are ten top tips to get the most out of cooking with a crock pot:

1. Cleaning your crock pot will be super easy and fast if you use a removable liner. Simply

tossing the liner after serving your meal is all there is to it: there's no need to soak or scrub the crock pot. You can get liners at most grocery stores. If you don't have any liners handy, use some nonstick cooking spray to make cleaning up easier.

2. On most crock pots, the "low" setting is about 200 degrees Fahrenheit, while "high" equals about 300 degrees Fahrenheit.

3. It's best not to put frozen food directly in a crock pot. This is because the temperature of the food should be brought to 140 degrees Fahrenheit as soon as possible and this won't work if you put frozen food in the pot. So defrost all food items first before placing them in the crock pot.

4. Don't peek when you are using the crock pot! If you lift the lid, the crock pot loses heat and steam and it takes around 15 to 20 minutes for it to reach the right temperature again.

5. By choosing either the "low" or "high" setting on the crock pot, you can make sure your meal is ready when you want it to be. One hour on "high" is about equivalent to 2 hours on "low".

6. Don't fill your crock pot all the way to the top with ingredients. Food will cook better when the crock pot is no more than 75% full.

7. Whole herbs gain extra flavor when they are cooked in a crock pot. Ground spices on the

other hand lose some of their flavor. So when you use ground spices for your recipe, add them during the last hour of cooking, or right before serving.

8. On the bottom of the crock pot, ingredients are cooked faster than on top. It is therefore usually best to put your meat and vegetables in first.

9. If you're adapting normal recipes for a crock pot, make sure to cut any liquids called for by the recipe by 1/3 to 1/2. In a crock pot, liquid does not evaporate as much as it does on a stovetop.

10. If you want to adapt your favorite stove/oven recipes to a crock pot, use the conversion table below.

Stove/Oven	Crock Pot LOW	Crock Pot HIGH
15-30 min	4-6 hours	1 ½ - 2 ½ hours
35-45 min	6-10 hours	3-4 hours
50-180 min	8-12 hours	4-6 hours

Breakfast Recipes

Chile Verde Breakfast Lasagna

Serves: 4
Total Time: 4 hours and 30 minutes
Equipment Needed: Crock pot, skillet

Ingredients:

- 1 pound bulk breakfast sausage
- ¾ cup sweet green pepper; finely chopped
- 1 jalapeno pepper; stemmed, seeded, and finely chopped
- 5 eggs beaten lightly
- 2 teaspoons vegetable oil
- ¼ cup green onions; sliced
- ¼ snipped cilantro or parsley
- ½ teaspoon salt
- ½ teaspoon cumin
- 9 gluten-free corn tortillas; 6 inch
- 2 cups Monterey jack cheese; shredded
- 1 16-ounce jar green salsa

Directions:

1. Lightly coat the inside of the slow cooker with nonstick cooking spray.

2. Brown sausage in skillet and drain off fat. Add the sweet pepper and jalapeno pepper to skillet and

cook over medium heat for 1 minute. Transfer sausage and peppers to bowl.

3. In the same pan cook eggs in hot oil just until set; stir to break up eggs. Combine eggs with sausage and peppers. Stir in green onions, cilantro, salt, and cumin.

4. Place 3 of the tortillas in the bottom of the slow cooker; it is fine if they overlap. Put half the egg and sausage mixture in the slow cooker and sprinkle with ½ cup of the cheese.

5. Pour 2/3 of the salsa over the mixture in the slow cooker. Continue layering until all tortillas, sausage mixture, and salsa are in the slow cooker.

6. Cover and set to low heat for 3 to 4 hours. Let stand for 15 minutes before serving. Can top with sour cream and cilantro if desired.

Nutritional Information:

Calories; 429, Fats 29 g, Carbohydrates 18 g, Protein 21 g, Sugar 3 g

Overnight Oatmeal

Serves: 4
Total Time: 9 hours and 10 minutes
Equipment Needed: Crock pot

Ingredients:

- 4 cups fat-free milk

- 4 cups water

- 2 cups gluten-free steel-cut oats

- 1/3 cup raisins

- 1/3 cup dried cherries

- 1/3 cup dried apricots, chopped

- 1 teaspoon molasses

- 1 teaspoon cinnamon (or pumpkin pie spice)

Directions:

1. In a slow cooker combine all of the ingredients. Turn heat to low.

2. Put the lid on and cook overnight for 8 to 9 hours.

3. Spoon into bowls and serve.

Nutrition Information:

Calories: 240 kcal, fat: 2.5 g; carbohydrates: 47 g; protein: 11 g

Breakfast Quinoa

Serves: 5
Total Time: 2 hours and 10 minutes
Equipment Needed: Crock pot; serving bowl

Ingredients:

- 1 cup quinoa
- 3 cups almond milk
- 1 apple (peeled; diced)
- 4 medjool dates (chopped)
- ¼ cup pepitas
- ¼ teaspoon nutmeg
- 2 teaspoons cinnamon powder
- 1 teaspoon pure vanilla extract
- ¼ teaspoon salt

Directions:

1. Place all the ingredients in a crock pot.

2. Allow it to cook on high heat for approximately 2 hours or until all the liquid has absorbed.

3. Serve!

Bacon and Spinach Quiche

Serves: 8

Total Time: 4 hours 10 minutes

Equipment needed: Crock pot and a mixing bowl

Ingredients:

- 10 eggs (beaten)
- 10 bacon slices (chopped)
- ½ cup spinach (chopped)
- 1 cup half and half
- 1 tablespoon butter
- 8 oz/225 g cheddar cheese (shredded)
- ½ teaspoon black pepper

Directions:

1. Grease the crock pot with butter. Set aside.

2. In a mixing bowl, whisk together the eggs with the cheese, half and half, spinach and pepper.

3. Pour the mixture into your crock pot and sprinkle the chopped bacon on top.

4. Allow it to cook on low heat for approximately 4 hours.

5. Serve!

Tater Tots Casserole

Serves: 8
Total Time: 8 hours 15 minutes
Equipment needed: Crock pot and a mixing bowl

Ingredients:

- 30 oz/850 g gluten-free Tater Tots

- 6 oz/170 g bacon (diced)

- 12 eggs

- 1 cup soy milk

- 2 onions (chopped)

- 4 tablespoons gluten-free all purpose flour

- 2 cups cheddar cheese (shredded)

- ¼ cup Parmesan cheese (grated)

- 1 teaspoon salt

- ½ teaspoon pepper

Directions:

1. Place one third of the tots in a greased crock pot followed by bacon, onions and cheese.

2. Layer them two more times in the same order with the cheese on top.

3. In a mixing bowl, combine the remaining ingredients and pour it in the crock pot.

Breakfast Recipes

4. Allow the tots to cook on low heat for approximately eight hours.

5. Serve!

Soups and Appetizers

Chicken Soup

Serves: 4
Total Time: 6 hours and 30 minutes
Equipment Needed: Crock pot, mixing bowl, and serving bowl

Ingredients:

- 3-4 chicken breasts

- 8 cloves fresh garlic, chopped

- Sea salt and freshly ground pepper, to taste

- 2 heaping cups cabbage (thinly shredded)

- 1 green bell pepper (deseeded, diced)

- 1 yellow summer squash (diced)

- 2 zucchini squash, cut up

- 6 to 8 baby potatoes cut up

- 1 4 oz/115 g can chopped green chilies

- 1 teaspoon sage

- 1 teaspoon each of: dried basil, oregano, and parsley

- 1 14 oz/400 g can diced tomatoes

- 2 or more cups gluten-free chicken broth, as needed

- A dash or two of balsamic vinegar to taste

- Olive oil, as needed

Directions:

1. Drizzle some olive oil into a slow cooker and lay the chicken breasts in it, with half the chopped garlic. Season a little with sea salt and pepper.

2. In a bowl, combine the bell pepper, shredded cabbage, zucchini squashes, potatoes, and green chilies, tossing them with another drizzle of olive oil. Season the mixture with sea salt, black pepper, herbs and toss to coat.

3. Pour the veggie mix into the crock in an even layer. Add in the tomatoes, chicken broth, and a small dash of balsamic vinegar, to taste.

4. The liquid content should just about cover the veggies in the pot. If you like, you can add more broth to get better consistency.

5. Cover the pot and let it cook for up to 5 to 6 hours, or until the chicken is tender and easily breaks apart into pieces.

Nutritional Information:

Calories: 277 kcal; Fats: 8.9 g; Carbohydrates: 13.6 g ; Protein: 35 g

Zucchini Soup

Serves: 4

Total Time: 3 hours and 30 minutes

Equipment Needed: Crock pot, chopping board, knife and serving bowl

Ingredients:

- 2 cups of chopped celery

- 2 pounds of zucchini, sliced

- 6 tomatoes, diced

- 2 green bell peppers, sliced

- 1 cup of chopped onion

- 2 teaspoons of salt

- 1 teaspoon of white sugar

- 1 teaspoon of oregano

- 1 teaspoon of Italian seasoning

- 1 teaspoon of basil

- ¼ teaspoon of garlic powder

- 6 tablespoons of shredded parmesan cheese

Directions:

1. Chop up everything that needs to get cut up and place in the slow cooker except for the cheese.

2. Stir well and put on high heat.

3. Cook for about three and a half hours.

4. Serve and enjoy with some of the shredded cheese on top.

Nutritional Information:

Calories: 389 kcal, Fats: 23.6 g, Carbohydrates: 25.8 g, Protein: 21.8 g

German Lentil Soup

Serves: 4
Total Time: 5 hours and 20 minutes
Equipment Needed: Crock pot, mixing bowl, and serving bowl

Ingredients:

- 2 cups of brown lentils
- 3 cups of gluten-free chicken broth
- 1 bay leaf
- 1 cup of carrots, chopped
- 1 cup of celery, chopped
- 1 cup of onion, chopped
- 1 teaspoon of gluten-free Worcestershire sauce
- ½ teaspoon of garlic powder
- ¼ teaspoon of nutmeg
- 5 drops of gluten-free hot sauce
- ¼ teaspoon of caraway seed
- ½ teaspoon of celery salt
- 1 tablespoon of parsley
- ½ teaspoon of pepper

Directions:

1. Cut up everything that needs to get cut up.

2. Place in the slow cooker and cook on high for about five hours.

3. Remove the bay leaf.

4. Serve and enjoy.

Nutritional Information:

Calories: 221 kcal, Fats: 2.3 g, Carbohydrates: 34.2 g, Protein: 16 g

Meatless Taco Soup

Serves: 4
Total Time: 3 hours and 45 minutes
Equipment Needed: Crock pot, chopping board, knife and serving bowl

Ingredients:

- 1 onion, chopped
- 1 can of chili beans
- 1 can of kidney beans
- 1 cup of corn
- 1 can of tomato sauce
- 2 cups of water
- 6 tomatoes, diced
- 2 green chili peppers
- 3 tablespoons of gluten-free taco seasoning mix

Directions:

1. Cut up everything that needs to be diced.

2. Place in the slow cooker and stir well.

3. Cook on high for about three and a half hours.

4. Serve and enjoy, try with some sour cream and shredded cheese on top.

Nutritional Information:

Calories: 362 kcal, Fats: 16.3 grams, Carbohydrates: 37.8 grams, Protein: 18.2 grams

Cabbage Soup

Serves: 4
Total Time: 4 hours and 15 minutes
Equipment Needed: Crock pot, chopping board, knife and serving bowl

Ingredients:

- 2 tablespoons of vegetable oil
- 1 onion, chopped
- 5 cups of cabbage, chopped
- 2 cans of red kidney beans
- 2 cups of water
- 6 cups of tomato sauce
- 4 tablespoons of seasoned salt
- 1 ½ teaspoons of cumin
- 1 teaspoon of salt
- 1 teaspoon of pepper

Directions:

1. Chop the cabbage and the onion up.

2. Place in slow cooker with everything else.

3. Cook on high for four hours.

4. Serve and enjoy!

Nutritional Information:

Calories: 211 kcal, Fats: 8.7 g, Carbohydrates: 20.3 g, Protein: 14.1 g

Green Curry Chicken Soup

Serves: 8
Total Time: 6 hours
Equipment Needed: Crock pot, mixing bowl, a spoon

Ingredients:

- 1 ½ can coconut milk (light)
- 3 tablespoons green curry paste
- 2½ lbs/1 kg chicken breast (cut into chunks)
- 1 can baby corn (drained)
- 2 tablespoons corn starch
- 3 tablespoons brown sugar
- 4 garlic cloves (minced)
- 1 bag stir fry vegetables (assorted)
- 1 red onion (sliced)

Directions:

1. Whisk together the coconut milk with the curry paste, garlic and brown sugar. Pour the mixture into the crock pot.

2. Add in the chicken, baby corn, onion and the assorted vegetables. Allow the soup to cook for four to five hours.

3. Next, mix the corn starch with approximately two tablespoons of water and add it to the crock pot.

4. Cook the mixture for an additional 30 minutes or so or until the soup thickens.

5. Serve hot!

Nutritional Information:

Calories: 240.9; Fat: 10.5 g; Protein: 35.5 g; Carbohydrates: 5.9 g

Chorizo and Chicken Soup

Serves: 8

Total Time: 4 hours

Equipment Needed: Crock pot, skillet, knife and serving bowl

Ingredients:

- 4 lbs/2 kg chicken thighs (boneless; skinless)

- 1 lb/500 g chorizo

- 1 can tomatoes (stewed)

- 4 cups chicken stock

- 2 tablespoons garlic (minced)

- 2 tablespoons gluten-free red hot sauce

- 2 tablespoons gluten-free Worcestershire sauce

- Shaved Parmesan (optional for garnishing)

- Sour cream (optional for garnishing)

Directions:

1. Heat the chorizo in a skillet until browned.

2. Place the chicken thighs in a crock pot followed by the chorizo and then the remaining ingredients.

3. Allow it to cook on high heat for approximately 3 hours.

4. After three hours are up, remove the chicken thighs, break apart and then return it back into the crock pot. Cook for an additional thirty minutes over low heat.

5. Garnish the soup with shaved Parmesan and sour cream before serving.

Nutritional Information:

Calories: 659; Fat: 47 g; Protein: 52 g; Carbohydrates: 6 g

French Onion Soup

Serves: 8
Total Time: 9 hours and 15 minutes
Equipment Needed: Crock pot, saucepan, and serving bowls

Ingredients:

- 4 sweet onions (sliced)
- 64 ounce vegetable or chicken broth
- 3 tablespoons gluten-free all purpose flour
- 2 tablespoons butter
- 1 tablespoon balsamic vinegar
- 1 tablespoon gluten-free Worcestershire sauce
- 2 tablespoons brown sugar
- 3 garlic cloves (minced)
- 2 tablespoons thyme
- ½ teaspoon pepper
- ½ teaspoon salt
- Low fat Swiss cheese (for garnishing; optional)

Directions:

1. Place the crock pot on the stove over high heat. Then add the onions, butter, vinegar, garlic, brown sugar, Worcestershire sauce, salt and pepper.

2. Allow it to cook for approximately an hour or until the onions turn brown and caramelize.

3. Next, stir in the flour and cook for an additional five minutes.

4. Finally, add the broth and the thyme and cook the soup on low heat for approximately six to eight hours.

5. Serve hot with a slice of Swiss cheese on top.

Nutritional Information:

Calories: 74.1; Fat: 3.7 g; Protein: 3.2 g; Carbohydrates: 7.4 g

Butternut Squash Soup

Serves: 6
Total Time: 8 hours and 20 minutes
Equipment Needed: Crock pot and a blender

Ingredients:

- 4 cups gluten-free chicken broth
- 1 medium butternut squash (peeled, seeded and chopped)
- 1 onion (chopped)
- 3 carrots (peeled and chopped)
- 3 garlic cloves (minced)
- 3 tablespoons Thai curry paste
- 1 tablespoon ginger (minced)
- 2 tablespoons maple syrup

Directions:

1. Place all the ingredients in a crock pot.

2. Cover and cook on low heat for approximately 6 to 8 hours or until the squash turns tender.

3. Using a hand blender blend the soup to get a smooth consistency and season it with salt and pepper.

4. Next, add half a cup of non-fat evaporated milk to make it extra creamy.

Nutritional Information:

Calories: 117; Fat: 18 g; Protein: 4.8 g; Carbohydrates: 12.6 g

Lunch Recipes

Greek Chicken and Vegetables

Serves: 6
Total Time: 3 hours and 20 minutes
Equipment Needed: Crock pot, knife, mixing bowl, spoon and serving bowl

Ingredients:

- 3 cups of baby carrots

- 1 pound of potatoes, cut into wedges

- 2 pounds of chicken thighs, skinless and boneless

- 1 can of gluten-free chicken broth, 14 ounces

- 1/3 cup of dry white wine

- 4 cloves of garlic, minced

- ¾ teaspoon of salt

- 1 can of artichoke hearts, 15 ounces

- 1 egg

- 2 egg yolks

- 1/3 cup of lemon juice

- 1/3 cup of dill

- 1 teaspoon of pepper

Directions:

1. Cut the potatoes and put on the bottom of the crock pot with the carrots.

Lunch Recipes

2. Put the chicken and the broth on top of the vegetables.

3. Cover with the wine and the salt.

4. Cut the garlic and add too.

5. Cook for three hours on high.

6. Open the can of artichokes, drain and add, cook for 5 minutes.

7. In the bowl combine the lemon juice, the egg, and the egg yolks.

8. Put the chicken in the serving bowl.

9. Add ½ cup of cooking liquid to the egg mixture, then put in the crock pot.

10. Stir with the pepper and the dill, cook for 15 minutes.

11. Pour sauce over the chicken and vegetables.

12. Serve and enjoy!

Nutritional Information:

Calories: 355 kcal Fats: 11 g; Carbohydrates: 27 g; Protein: 34 g

Chickpea Curry

Serves: 4
Total Time: 5 hours and 40 minutes
Equipment Needed: Crock pot, paper towels, pan

Ingredients:

- 2 cups cauliflower florets; small

- 2 cups peeled and cubed sweet potato

- 1 cup onion; chopped

- 1 tablespoon curry powder

- 1 tablespoon brown sugar

- 1 tablespoon grated ginger

- 1 ¼ teaspoon salt

- 2 minced garlic cloves

- 1 can chickpeas; drained and rinsed (16 oz/450 g)

- 1 can no salt diced tomatoes; un-drained (14.5 oz/400 g)

- 1 can coconut milk (light) (13.5 oz/380 g)

- 1 package extra-firm tofu; drained (14 oz/400 g)

- 1 tablespoon canola oil

- 3 cups cooked rice

- 3 tablespoons chopped cilantro; fresh

Directions:

1. Combine first 11 ingredients in slow cooker and stir well. Cover and cook on low setting for 5.5 hours or until vegetables are tender.

2. Place tofu on layers of paper towels and cover with additional towels. Press down to absorb excess liquid and cut into ½ cubes.

3. Heat oil in pan and cook tofu for 8 to 10 minutes or until browned. Stir into mixture in slow cooker.

4. Serve over rice and garnish with cilantro.

Nutritional Information:

Calories; 328, Fats 7 g, Carbohydrates 11 g, Protein 12.8 g

Risotto with Fennel

Serves: 4
Total Time: 3 hours and 45 minutes
Equipment Needed: Crock pot, chopping board, knife and serving platter

Ingredients:

- 2 teaspoons of fennel seeds

- 1 fennel bulb, cored and diced

- 1 cup of brown rice

- 1 carrot, chopped

- 1 shallot, chopped

- 2 cloves of garlic, minced

- 4 cups of gluten-free chicken broth

- 1 ½ cups of water

- 1/3 cup of dry white wine

- 2 cups of green beans

- ½ cup of shredded parmesan cheese

- 1/3 cup of pitted black olives, chopped

- 1 tablespoon of grated lemon zest

- ½ teaspoon of salt

- ½ teaspoon of pepper

Directions:

1. Chop the carrot, the shallot, the black olives and core and chop the fennel bulb.

2. Grate the lemon zest and mince the garlic.

3. Place all of the ingredients into the slow cooker and stir until well mixed.

4. Cook for three and a half hours on low.

5. Stir and cook until desired heat is cooked all the way through.

6. Serve and enjoy, try some parmesan cheese on top.

Nutritional Information:

Calories: 242 kcal, Fats: 6 g, Carbohydrates: 36 g, Protein: 10 g

Slow cooked beans

Serves: 4
Total Time: 4 hours and 30 minutes
Equipment Needed: Crock pot, chopping board, knife and serving bowl

Ingredients:

- 1 pound of dried beans, mix pinto beans with black beans and kidney beans
- 1 onion, chopped
- 4 cloves of garlic, minced
- 1 teaspoon of thyme
- 1 bay leaf
- 5 cups of boiling water
- ½ teaspoon of salt

Directions:

1. Place the beans in a large pot with the water, bring to a boil on high heat and cook for about one hour.

2. Drain the beans.

3. Chop the onion and mince the garlic.

4. Add to the beans along with the bay leaf and thyme. Stir well.

5. Lower heat and cook for about three more hours.

Lunch Recipes

6. Add the salt and cook for 15 more minutes.

7. Serve and enjoy.

Nutritional Information:

Calories: 260 kcal, Fats: 1 g, Carbohydrates: 48 g, Protein: 15 g

Refried Beans

Serves: 4
Total Time: 5 hours and 20 minutes
Equipment Needed: Crock pot, chopping board, knife

Ingredients:

- 1 onion, chopped
- 3 cups of pinto beans
- ¼ cup of chopped jalapeno pepper
- 2 tablespoons of minced garlic
- 5 teaspoons of salt
- ¾ teaspoon of pepper
- 1/8 teaspoon of cumin
- 9 cups of water

Directions:

1. Chop up the onion and place in the slow cooker with everything else.

2. Cook on high for about five hours.

3. Once the beans are cooked, strain them and mash them.

4. Serve and enjoy!

Nutritional Information;

Calories: 139 kcal, Fats: 0.5 g, Carbohydrates: 25.4 g, Protein: 8.5 g

Tofu Curry

Serves: 4
Total Time: 4 hours and 20 minutes
Equipment Needed: Crock pot, chopping board, knife

Ingredients:

- 1 pound tofu (firm; cubed)

- 2 cups sweet corn

- 15 oz/425 g coconut milk

- ¼ cup curry paste

- 2 cups vegetable stock

- 6 oz/170 g tomato paste (canned)

- 1 yellow pepper (chopped)

- 1 red pepper (chopped)

- 1 sweet onion (chopped)

- 3 garlic cloves (minced)

- 2 gingers (minced)

- 1 tablespoon gluten-free garam masala

- 1 teaspoon low salt

- Cilantro (for garnishing)

Directions:

1. Start by cutting the tofu into ½ inch cubes and add it to a large slow cooker.

2. Next, add the chopped onion, peppers, ginger and garlic to the slow cooker as well followed by the corn, vegetable stock, tomato paste, coconut milk, curry paste, and spices.

3. Stir well! Then cover and allow the curry to cook on high heat for approximately 3 to 4 hours.

4. Garnish it with cilantro and serve over brown rice or as desired.

Nutritional Information:

Calories: 328 kcal, Fats: 7 g, Carbohydrates: 53.8 g, Protein: 12.8 g

Chicken Tikka Masala

Serves: 6
Total Time: 4 hours and 20 minutes
Equipment Needed: Crock pot and a mixing bowl

Ingredients:

- 2 lbs/1 kg chicken thighs (boneless; skinless)
- 28 oz/800 g canned tomatoes (crushed)
- 1 tablespoon garlic (minced)
- 2 tablespoons gluten-free garam masala
- 1 tablespoon kosher salt
- 1 tablespoon ginger root (minced)
- 1 onion (chopped)
- ½ teaspoon ground cumin
- ½ teaspoon ground coriander
- 1 tablespoon brown sugar
- ½ cup Greek yogurt (fat free)
- ¼ cup cilantro (chopped)

Directions:

1. In a mixing bowl, combine the crushed tomatoes with garam masala, garlic, ginger, sugar, cumin, coriander and salt.

2. Pour the mixture into the crock pot.

3. Now add the onions and the chicken to the crock pot.

4. Cook on high heat for approximately four hours.

5. After the four hours are up add the yogurt to the chicken and mix well.

6. Top it off with cilantro and serve!

Nutritional Information:

Calories: 329 kcal, Fats: 17 g, Carbohydrates: 15.8 g, Protein: 29.6 g

Lentil and Mushroom Stew

Serves: 4

Total Time: 4 hours and 30 minutes

Equipment Needed: Crock pot, chopping board, knife

Ingredients:

- 2 quarts of gluten-free vegetable broth
- 2 cups of mushrooms, sliced
- 1 ounce of shiitake mushrooms, chopped
- ¾ cup of lentils
- ¼ cup of onion flakes
- 2 teaspoons of minced garlic
- 2 teaspoons of pepper
- 3 bay leaves

- 1 teaspoon of basil
- 1 teaspoon of salt

Directions:

1. Cut up everything and place in crock pot.

2. Stir well and cook on high heat for four hours.

3. Remove bay leaves.

4. Serve and enjoy!

Nutritional Information:

Calories: 213 kcal, Fats: 1.2 g, Carbohydrates: 43.9 g, Protein: 8.4 g

Pumpkin Goulash

Serves: 6
Total Time: 4 hours and 30 minutes
Equipment Needed: Crock pot, chopping board, knife

Ingredients:

- 6 diced tomatoes

- 1 tablespoon of brown sugar

- 2 tablespoons of olive oil

- 1 onion, chopped

- 1 teaspoon of ginger

- 1 teaspoon of cinnamon

- 1 teaspoon of cumin

- 1 tablespoon of coriander

- 1 can of garbanzo beans

- 3 pounds of fresh pumpkin, peeled and cut into small chunks

- 1 teaspoon of salt

- 1 teaspoon of cornstarch

- ¼ cup of water

Directions:

1. Peel and cut the pumpkin up.

2. Chop up everything else that needs to get cut up.

3. Place it all in the crock pot.

4. Cook on high heat for about four hours.

5. Serve and enjoy!

Nutritional Information:

Calories: 330 kcal, Fats: 7.9 g, Carbohydrates: 37.2 g, Protein: 28.4 g

Eggplant Sauce

Serves: 2
Total Time: 8 hours and 20 minutes
Equipment Needed: Crock pot, chopping board, knife

Ingredients:

- 1 eggplant

- 2 14.5 oz/400 g cans diced tomatoes

- 6 oz/170 g tomato paste (canned)

- 1 4 oz/110 g can sliced mushrooms; drained

- ¼ cup red wine (dry)

- ¼ cup water

- ½ cup onion (chopped)

- 2 cloves of garlic (chopped)

- 1½ teaspoon oregano

- 1/3 cup olives (pitted)

- 2 tablespoons fresh parsley; chopped

- Parmesan cheese (shredded; optional)

Directions:

1. Peel eggplant and cut into small cubes.

2. In the slow cooker combine the eggplant, onion, canned tomatoes with juice, tomato paste, mushrooms, wine, water, garlic, and oregano.

3. Cover the slow cooker and allow it to cook on low heat for approximately 7 to 8 hours.

4. Add the olives and parsley.

5. Serve over cooked rice and sprinkle with Parmesan cheese.

Nutritional Information:

Calories; 346, Fats 4 g, Carbohydrates 65 g, Protein 13 g, Sugar 5 g

Chipotle Beef Tacos with Cabbage and Radish Slaw

Serves: 4
Total Time: 4 hours and 30 minutes
Equipment Needed: Crock pot, oven, bowl and a fork

Ingredients:

- 3 pounds beef; trimmed and cut into 2 inch cubes
- 1 large onion; sliced thin
- 4 chopped cloves of garlic
- 1 to 3 tablespoons chopped chipotle; canned in adobo sauce
- 1 teaspoon oregano
- 2 bay leaves
- Kosher salt
- 4 cups cabbage; thinly sliced
- 4 radishes (halved and thinly sliced)
- ¼ cup fresh cilantro
- 2 tablespoons lime juice
- Corn tortillas
- Toppings: sour cream, salsa, jalapenos, shredded cheese

Directions:

1. In the slow cooker toss together the beef, garlic, onion, chipotles, oregano, bay leaves, cilantro, and salt (tip: add just a bit of water to bottom to avoid sticking).

2. Cook on high for 3.5 to 4 hours.

3. Twenty minutes before meat mixture is done wrap tortillas in foil and place in 350 degree oven for 5 to ten minutes to warm.

4. While tortillas are warming and meat is finishing up, toss together the cabbage, radishes, lime juice, and ¼ teaspoon salt.

5. Transfer the meat to a bowl and shred with a fork; save the broth. Strain the liquid into the meat and stir to combine.

6. Fill tortillas with beef and slaw; top with your choice of toppings.

Nutritional Information:

Calories; 521, Fats 6 g, Carbohydrates 34 g, Protein 57 g, Sugar 5 g

Smoky Slow Cooker Chili

Serves: 6
Total Time: 5 hours and 30 minutes
Equipment Needed: Crock pot, skillet, serving bowls

Ingredients:

- 1 pound ground pork
- 1 pound pork shoulder; trimmed and cut into ½ inch cubes
- 1 ¾ cup bell pepper; chopped
- 3 minced cloves of garlic
- 3 tablespoons tomato paste
- 1 cup gluten-free (ginger) beer
- 3 tablespoons chili powder
- 1 tablespoon cumin
- 2 teaspoons oregano
- ¾ teaspoon black pepper
- 6 quarter tomatillos
- 2 bay leaves
- 2 14.5 oz/400 g cans plum tomatoes; chopped and drained
- 1 15 oz/425 g can pinto beans drained; no salt added
- 1 7.75 oz/220 g can Mexican style tomato sauce
- 1 smoked ham hock

- 1 ½ tablespoon sugar
- ½ cup cilantro; chopped finely
- ½ cup green onion; chopped finely
- ½ cup crumbled queso fresco
- 8 lime wedges

Directions:

1. Brown pork in skillet and transfer to crock pot after draining fat.

2. In skillet sprayed with nonstick spray sauté onion and bell pepper for 8 minutes; stirring often. Add garlic and sauté 1 minute more. Add tomato paste and cook for 1 minute; stirring constantly. Stir in gluten-free beer and continue cooking for 1 minute. Add onion mixture to slow cooker with meat.

3. Add chili powder, cumin, oregano, pepper, tomatillos, bay leaves, plum tomatoes, beans, tomato sauce, and ham hock. Cover and set crock pot on high for 5 hours.

4. Remove bay leaves and ham hock; discard. Stir in sugar.

5. Ladle into serving cups or bowls; top with 1 tablespoon cilantro, cheese, green onions, and serve with a lime wedge.

Nutritional Information:

Calories; 357, Fats 14.4 g, Carbohydrates 26 g, Protein 27.7 g

Chicken Enchilada Stack

Serves: 6
Total Time: 2 hours and 30 minutes
Equipment Needed: Crock pot, skillet, blender

Ingredients:

- 1 teaspoon canola oil

- 1 cup onion; chopped

- ½ cup poblano, seeded and chopped

- 2 minced cloves garlic

- 1 ½ teaspoon chipotle chili powder

- 1 14.5 oz/400 g can diced tomatoes; drained and no salt added

- 1 8 oz/225 g can tomato sauce; Italian seasoned

- Cooking spray

- 2 cups rotisserie chicken breast; shredded

- 1 cup frozen; white and yellow corn

- 1 15 oz/425 g can black beans; drained and rinsed

- 5 gluten-free corn tortillas

- 8 oz/225 g shredded cheddar cheese; reduced fat

- Cilantro sprigs

Directions:

1. Using a nonstick skillet heat on medium and add oil. Add onion, pepper, and garlic; cook until tender; about 6 minutes

2. Stir in chili powder, tomatoes, and tomato sauce. Put half the tomato mixture in a blender. Remove lid of blender and let steam escape. Place a towel over blender and blend until almost smooth and pour into a bowl. Repeat process with the other half of tomato mixture.

3. Spray slow cooker with nonstick cooking spray. Spread 3 tablespoons of tomato mixture on bottom of slow cooker. Mix the remainder of tomato mixture with chicken, corn, and beans.

4. Place one tortilla on the tomato mixture in the slow cooker. Cover with 1 cup of chicken mixture. Sprinkle with cheese; about 1/3 cup. Top with another tortilla and repeat process until all tortillas and chicken mixture are in slow cooker.

5. Cook on low setting for 2 hours or until the cheese is melted and the edges are browned.

6. Garnish it with cilantro and serve!

Nutritional Information:

Calories; 295, Fats 10.3 g, Carbohydrates 16 g, Protein 24 g

Chicken and Broccoli Casserole

Serves: 4
Total Time: 4 hours
Equipment needed: A crock pot

Ingredients:

- 1 pound broccoli (frozen)
- 1 pound boiled chicken (cut into chunks)
- 1 cup gluten-free chicken broth
- ½ tablespoon cream
- ½ pound cream cheese
- ½ pound shredded cheese

Directions:

1. Place all the ingredients in a slow cooker and allow it to cook for approximately 3 to 4 hours on low heat.

2. Serve hot!

Nutritional Information:

Calories: 405, Fats: 46.8 g, Carbohydrates: 15.2 g, Protein: 56.2 g

Beef and Cheese Casserole

Serves: 6
Total Time: 11 hours 40 minutes
Equipment Needed: A crock pot

Ingredients:

- 1 lb/500 g ground beef (browned and drained)
- 1 can of gluten-free cream of mushroom soup
- 1 cup canned corn (drained)
- 1 can diced tomatoes (with liquid)
- ¼ cup onion (diced)
- 1 lb/500 g red potatoes (sliced thinly)
- 1 can dark kidney beans (drained)
- 1 cup cheese (shredded)
- 1 teaspoon salt
- ½ teaspoon pepper
- ½ teaspoon Mrs. Dash

Ingredients:

1. Place all the ingredients except for the cheese in a slow cooker. Mix well.

2. Cover and cook on high heat for four hours.

3. After the first four hours are up, cook for an additional seven hours on low heat.

4. Remove the cover and sprinkle the cheese on top.

5. Cover it again and cook for an additional 30 minutes before serving.

Nutritional Information:

Calories: 374, Fats: 28.6 g, Carbohydrates: 14.3 g, Protein: 33 g

Beef Goulash

Serves: 4
Total Time: 5 hours and 20 minutes
Equipment Needed: Crock pot, mixing bowl, saucepan

Ingredients:

- 12 oz/340 g beef round steak (cubed)

- 1 cup gluten-free beef stock (unsalted)

- 2 cups onion (diced)

- 8 cups red cabbage (shredded)

- ¼ cup tomato paste

- 14 oz/400 g canned tomatoes with garlic and green chili pepper (diced)

- ½ cup avocado (seeded; diced)

- 2 garlic cloves (minced)

- 1 bay leaf

- 2 tablespoons paprika

- 1 tablespoon walnuts (toasted; crushed)

- 1 teaspoon fennel seeds

- ½ cup cranberry raspberry sauce

- 2 tablespoons lime juice

- ½ teaspoon sea salt

- ¼ teaspoon black pepper

- 1 cup water

Directions:

1. Place the onions, meat, bay leaf and garlic in a crock pot.

2. In a mixing bowl, combine the broth with the tomatoes, tomato paste, fennel seeds, paprika, pepper and salt.

3. Stir the mixture into the slow cooker. Cover and cook on high heat for approximately 4 to 5 hours.

4. In a saucepan, boil the water. Add in the cabbage and cook over medium heat for approximately 5-7 minutes or until it becomes tender. Then add in the avocado and lime.

5. Divide the berry sauce equally among four dishes and garnish it with nuts.

6. Next divide the cabbage into four soup bowls. Top it off with the cooked Goulash and Avocado mixture.

7. Serve!

Nutritional Information:

Calories 355; Fat 11 g; Carbohydrates 38 g; Protein 25 g

Teriyaki Pork Tenderloin

Serves: 8
Total Time: 4 hours 40 minutes
Equipment needed: A crock pot, a skillet and a mixing bowl

Ingredients:

- 2 pounds pork tenderloin
- 1 cup gluten-free chicken broth
- ¼ cup brown sugar
- ½ cup teriyaki sauce
- ½ onion (sliced)
- 4 garlic cloves (chopped)
- 3 red chili peppers (chopped)
- ¼ teaspoon black pepper
- 2 tablespoons olive oil (extra virgin)

Directions:

1. In a skillet, heat the oil over medium high heat.

2. Add the tenderloins to the skillet and cook for approximately 10 minutes or until it turns brown on all sides.

3. In a mixing bowl, combine the broth with the sauce, sugar, peppers, onion and garlic.

4. Now place the tenderloins in the crock pot and top it off with the teriyaki mixture.

Lunch Recipes

5. Cook the tenderloins on high heat for approximately 4 hours or until well done.

6. Allow it to cool for 3-5 minutes before slicing.

Nutritional Information:

Calories 175; Fat 6.1 g; Carbohydrates 10.1 g; Protein 19.1 g

Dinner Recipes

Thai Chicken Curry

Serves: 4
Total time: 3 hours 20 minutes
Equipment needed: Mixing bowl and a crock pot

Ingredients:

- 4 chicken thighs
- 1 teaspoon red curry powder
- 1 teaspoon red curry paste
- 14 ounce coconut milk
- 1 cup snap peas
- 2 tablespoons peanut butter
- ½ sweet onion (chopped)
- ½ cup cilantro (chopped)
- 1 teaspoon basil (dried)
- ½ red bell pepper (chopped)
- 2 tablespoons liquid amino acid
- 1/8 teaspoon red pepper flakes
- ½ teaspoon brown sugar

Directions:

1. In a mixing bowl, whisk together the coconut milk with the curry powder, curry paste, brown sugar, peanut butter, liquid amino acid, pepper flakes and basil.

2. Pour the mixture into a crock pot.

3. Add the onions, bell pepper and cilantro and stir.

4. Next add the chicken and allow it to cook on high heat for approximately 3 hours.

5. After the 3 hours are up, stir in the peas and cook for an additional 10 minutes.

6. Serve!

Nutritional Information:

Calories: 434 kcal, Fats: 34.9 g, Carbohydrates: 11.9 g, Protein: 22.2 g

Pineapple Chicken

Serves: 4
Total Time: 4 hours 20 minutes
Equipment needed: Shallow dish, mixing bowl and a crock pot

Ingredients:

- 4 chicken thighs (trimmed)
- 1 cup gluten-free all purpose flour
- 1 cup pineapple chunks
- ¾ cup fresh pineapple juice
- 2 tablespoons ketchup
- ½ cup gluten-free soy sauce
- 1/3 cup brown sugar
- 1 garlic clove (minced)

Directions:

1. In a shallow bowl, dredge the chicken in the flour to coat it completely.

2. Next, place the chicken in the crock pot and top it off with pineapple.

3. In a mixing bowl, whisk together the rest of the ingredients.

4. Pour it over the chicken and the pine apple.

5. Allow the chicken to cook on low heat for approximately four hours.

6. Serve!

Nutritional Information:

Calories: 448 kcal, Fats: 11.7 g, Carbohydrates: 62.2 g, Protein: 23.6 g

Beef Vegetable Stew

Serves: 4
Total Time: 5 hours 30 minutes
Equipment needed: Shallow dish; cooking pot and a crock pot

Ingredients:

- 2 lbs/1 kg grass-fed beef (organic; cubed)
- 4 cups gluten-free beef broth (organic)
- 3 gold potatoes (peeled; sliced)
- 3 carrots (peeled; sliced)
- 2 celery stalks (sliced)
- 5 garlic cloves (chopped)

- 1 cup pearl onions (trimmed; peeled)
- 1 cup red wine (dry)
- 2 teaspoons Italian herbs (dried)
- 1 bay leaf
- 2 tablespoons olive oil (extra virgin)
- Sea salt (to taste)
- Ground pepper (to taste)

Directions:

1. In a shallow dish marinade the beef with salt. Set aside.

2. In a pot, heat the olive oil over medium high heat.

3. Place the beef cubes in the pot and allow it to cook over medium high heat for five to seven minutes or until the beef turns brown.

4. Remove the beef and place it at the bottom of the crock pot.

5. Now add the vegetables along with the broth and the wine. Stir gently and add the herbs and ground pepper.

6. Cover and cook for approximately 4 to 5 hours on high heat.

7. Serve!

Nutritional Information:

Calories: 321, Fats: 22.8 g, Carbohydrates: 17.1 g, Protein: 34 g

Mexican Chuck Roast

Serves: 12
Total Time: 10 hours 10 minutes
Equipment needed: A skillet and a crock pot

Ingredients:

- 4 pounds chuck roast

- 1 onion (chopped)

- 1 ¼ cup green chili pepper (diced)

- 5 ounce gluten-free hot pepper sauce

- 1 teaspoon ground black pepper

- 1 teaspoon salt

- 1 teaspoon chili powder

- 1 teaspoon garlic powder

- 1 teaspoon cayenne pepper

- 2 tablespoons olive oil

Directions:

1. Start by seasoning the roast with salt and pepper.

2. Next, in a large skillet heat the olive oil over medium high heat and cook the beef until it turns brown.

3. Transfer the beef into the crock pot. Top it off with onions and pepper.

4. Now add the hot pepper sauce, chili powder, cayenne pepper and garlic powder.

5. Add water so that it covers one third of the roast.

6. Cook on high heat for approximately 6 hours and then reduce the heat to low and continue cooking for another 3 to 4 hours or until the beef shreds and falls apart.

7. Serve in gluten-free tacos!

Nutritional Information:

Calories: 260 kcal, Fats: 19.1 g, Carbohydrates: 3.3 g, Protein: 18.4 g

Cranberry Pork

Serves: 6
Total Time: 4 hours 10 minutes
Equipment needed: Mixing bowl and a crock pot

Ingredients:

- 3 pound pork loin roast (boneless)

- 16 ounce cranberry sauce

- 1 onion (sliced)

- 1/3 cup gluten-free salad dressing (French)

Directions:

1. In a mixing bowl, whisk together the cranberry sauce with the French salad dressing and the onion.

2. Place the pork loin in the crock pot and top it off with the cranberry mixture.

3. Allow the pork to cook on high heat for approximately 4 hours.

4. Serve!

Nutritional Information:

Calories: 374 kcal, Fats: 15.1 g, Carbohydrates: 32.9 g, Protein: 26.8 g

Thanksgiving Style Turkey Legs

Serves: 6
Total Time: 8 hours 10 minutes
Equipment needed: Aluminum foil, mixing bowl and a crock pot

Ingredients:

- 6 turkey legs (washed)

- Salt and pepper (to taste)

- 3 teaspoons gluten-free poultry seasoning

Directions:

1. Place the turkey legs in a medium bowl. Marinade it with salt, pepper and poultry seasoning.

2. Wrap the legs in the aluminum foil and place it into the crock pot.

3. Allow it to cook for approximately 7 to 8 hours over low heat.

4. Serve!

Nutritional Information:

Calories: 217 kcal, Fats: 6.9 g, Carbohydrates: 0.2 g, Protein: 36.3 g

Orange Chicken

Serves: 4
Total Time: 6 hours 20 minutes
Equipment needed: A crock pot

Ingredients:

- 1 pound chicken breast (boneless, halved)
- 12 ounce orange flavored beverage
- ½ cup gluten-free soy sauce

Directions:

1. Place the chicken breasts in the crock pot. Top it off with the orange beverage and soy sauce.

2. Allow the chicken to cook on low heat for approximately five to six hours.

3. Serve with brown rice.

Nutritional Information:

Calories: 357 kcal, Fats: 2.7 g, Carbohydrates: 0.53 g, Protein: 27.8 g

Beef Chili

Serves: 6
Total Time: 8 hours 10 minutes
Equipment needed: A crock pot

Ingredients:

- 1 lb/500 g ground beef (browned and drained)
- 14 oz/400 g gluten-free beef broth
- 1 cup chopped onion
- 3 stalks of celery
- 2 garlic cloves (minced)
- 1 8 oz/225 g can tomato sauce
- 1 14 oz/400 g can diced tomatoes (with juice)
- 1 cup water (hot)
- 1 ½ teaspoon chili powder
- ½ teaspoon cumin
- ½ teaspoon paprika
- ½ teaspoon oregano
- 1 teaspoon salt
- 1 teaspoon black pepper
- A dash of cayenne pepper

Directions:

1. Put a crock pot on low heat.

2. Add all the ingredients to it. Cover and allow it to cook for approximately six to eight hours on low heat.

Nutritional Information:

Calories: 59; Fat: 9 g; Protein: 4.4 g; Carbohydrates: 1.6 g

Squash Quinoa Casserole

Serves: one casserole
Total Time: 4 hours and 15 minutes
Equipment Needed: Crock pot, chopping board, knife

Ingredients:

- 12 ounces of tomatillos, de-husked and chopped
- 1 pint of cherry tomatoes, chopped
- 1 bell pepper, chopped
- ½ cup of chopped onion
- 1 tablespoon of lime juice
- 1 teaspoon of salt
- 1 cup of quinoa
- 1 cup of feta cheese
- 2 pounds of yellow squash, sliced
- 2 tablespoons of oregano

Directions:

1. Chop everything up that needs to get cut.

2. Place everything in the crock pot and cook on low for four hours.

3. Serve and enjoy.

Nutritional Information:

Calories: 111 kcal, Fats: 3 g, Carbohydrates: 18 g, Protein: 5 g

Pinto Bean Sloppy Joe Mix

Serves: 4
Total Time: 5 hours
Equipment Needed: Crock pot, chopping board, knife

Ingredients:

- 2 tablespoons of olive oil

- 2 carrots, sliced

- 1 onion, sliced

- 4 cloves of garlic, minced

- 3 tablespoons of chili powder

- 2 tablespoons of balsamic vinegar

- 1 cup of pinto beans

- 1 red bell pepper, diced

- 8 ounces of tomato sauce

- ½ cup of water

- 2 tablespoons of gluten-free soy sauce

- 2 tablespoons of tomato paste

- 4 cups of green cabbage, sliced

- 1 zucchini, chopped

- 1 cup of corn

- 3 tablespoons of honey mustard

- 1 tablespoon of brown sugar

- 1 teaspoon of salt

- 10 lettuce leaves

Directions:

1. Cut up everything that needs to get cut up and place in slow cooker.

2. Cook on high heat for 5 hours with the other ingredients.

3. Place the cabbage and the zucchini in the last 30 minutes.

4. Serve on lettuce and enjoy.

Nutritional Information:

Calories: 283 kcal, Fats: 6 g, Carbohydrates: 51 g, Protein: 11 g

Turkey stew with green chilies

Serves: 5
Total Time: 4 hours and 30 minutes
Equipment Needed: Crock pot, skillet, serving bowl

Ingredients:

- 1 ½ cups butternut squash (peeled and diced)
- 1 lb/500 g ground turkey
- 2 large potatoes (peeled and diced)
- 3 medium carrots (peeled and chopped)
- 1 onion (diced)
- 4 cloves garlic (minced)
- 1 teaspoon cumin
- 1 teaspoon chili powder
- 1 cup roasted chopped green chili
- 1 quart gluten-free chicken stock
- Low salt and black pepper to taste

For serving:
- Juice from 1 lime
- 2-3 tablespoons chopped cilantro
- 1-2 teaspoons agave nectar, as needed

Directions:

1. First, brown the ground turkey in a skillet and take out the excess fat, if any.

2. Now add the turkey to the slow cooker with the remaining ingredients up to salt and black pepper. Stir well to combine.

3. Cover and cook until the pork is done.

4. About 20 minutes before serving, stir in the lime juice and cilantro. Add some sweetener, if needed, to balance out the spice and if you need a little more liquid, add more broth to it and heat through.

Nutritional information:

Calories: 423 kcal; Fats: 13.5 g; Carbohydrates: 44.7 g; Protein: 36.3 g

Spicy Spinach Sauce

Serves: 4
Total Time: 6 hours and 30 minutes
Equipment Needed: Crock pot, spoon and mixing bowl

Ingredients:

- 28 ounce canned tomatoes (peeled and crushed)

- 10 ounce frozen spinach (chopped, thawed and drained)

- 1 onion (chopped)

- 1/3 cup carrot (grated)

- 2 ½ tablespoons red pepper (crushed)

- 5 garlic cloves (minced)

- 6 ounce canned tomato paste

- 4.5 ounce canned mushrooms (sliced and drained)

- 2 tablespoons dried oregano

- 2 tablespoons salt

- 2 tablespoons dried basil

- 2 bay leaves

- ¼ cup olive oil (extra virgin)

Directions:

1. Combine olive oil with spinach, onion, garlic, carrots, tomato paste and mushrooms in a 5 quart crock pot.

2. Add in the salt, pepper, oregano, bay leaves, basil and tomatoes.

3. Cover and cook for approximately 4 hours over high heat. After 4 hours are up, stir and reduce the heat to low and cook for an additional 2 hours.

Nutritional Information:

Calories; 176, Fats 8.2 g, Carbohydrates 25.1 g, Protein 6.6 g

Slow Cooker Cassoulet

Serves: 4
Total Time: 9 hours and 15 minutes
Equipment Needed: Crock pot, a large skillet, mixing bowl, and serving bowl

Ingredients:

- 1 pound navy beans (dry; soaked overnight)
- 4 cups gluten-free mushroom broth
- 1 cube gluten-free vegetable bouillon
- 1 onion
- 2 carrots (peeled and diced)
- 1 potato (peeled and cubed)
- 4 sprigs of parsley
- 1 sprig of rosemary
- 1 sprig of lemon thyme (chopped)
- 1 sprig of savory
- 1 bay leaf
- 2 tablespoons olive oil (extra virgin)

Directions:

1. In a large skillet, heat the oil over medium heat. Stir in the onion and the carrots and cook until it becomes tender.

2. In a crock pot, combine the beans with the broth, bouillon, carrots, onion and bay leaf. Add in half a cup of water if required.

3. Season the mixture with parsley, thyme, rosemary and savory and allow it to cook on low heat for approximately 8 hours or so.

4. Next, stir in the potato and continue to cook for another hour.

5. Remove all the herbs and serve!

Nutritional Information:

Calories; 279, Fats 4.4 g, Carbohydrates 47.2 g, Protein 15.3 g

Hash brown Casserole with Mushrooms

Serves: 6
Total Time: 10 hours 20 minutes
Equipment needed: A crock pot and 3 mixing bowls

Ingredients:

- 10 oz/285 g frozen gluten-free hash browns

- 10 oz/285 g frozen spinach (defrosted and drained)

- 4 oz/115 g chopped ham

- 4 eggs

- 8 egg whites

- 1 bell pepper (diced)

- ¼ cup onions (diced)

- 1 cup cheddar cheese (shredded)

- ½ cup soy milk

- ½ teaspoon salt

- ¼ teaspoon pepper

Directions:

1. Start by spraying some cooking spray in your slow cooker.

2. Next, in a mixing bowl, mix the hash browns with onions and peppers and place it at the bottom of your slow cooker. Season it with salt and pepper.

3. In another mixing bowl, mix the spinach together with the ham.

4. Layer the slow cooker with half of the spinach and ham mix. Then cover it with half a cup of cheese. Now layer the additional vegetables on top followed by the remaining cheese.

5. In a separate mixing bowl, whisk together the eggs, egg whites, salt, pepper and the milk. Pour the egg mixture on top of the cheese in the slow cooker.

6. Cover and cook on high heat for approximately 4 hours and then on low heat for an additional 6-8 hours.

Nutritional Information:

Calories; 275, Fats 18.3 g, Carbohydrates 11.9 g, Protein 20.8 g

Pollo Pibil

Serves: 8
Total Time: 5 hours
Equipment needed: A crock pot, blender and a bowl

Ingredients:

- 3 lbs/1.5 kg chicken thighs (boneless)

- 2 habaneros (seeded and diced)

- ¼ cup chicken broth

- 4 tablespoons achiote paste

- ½ cup orange juice

- ½ cup apple cider vinegar

- 1 onion (chopped)

- 1 teaspoon coriander

- 1 teaspoon cumin

- 1 teaspoon oregano (dried)

- 3 garlic cloves (diced)

- Salt and pepper (to taste)

Directions:

1. Season the chicken with salt and pepper. Set it aside for an hour.

2. In a blender combine all the remaining ingredients to form a thick sauce-like mixture.

3. Now place the chicken into the slow cooker and pour the mixture on top of the chicken.

4. Cover and cook for at least four hours or until the chicken can be easily shredded.

5. Shred the chicken and allow it to cook for another 30 minutes more with the lid off so that the sauce thickens.

6. Serve!

Nutritional Information:

Calories: 139.8; Fat: 4.1 g; Protein: 20.8 g; Carbohydrates: 3.8 g

Rabbit Stew

Serves: 6
Total Time: 6 hours 20 minutes
Equipment needed: A crock pot and a skillet

Ingredients:

- 1 3 lb/1.5 kg rabbit (cut into pieces)

- ½ lb/250 g smoked pork belly (cut into cubes)

- 2 cups white wine (dry)

- 2 tablespoons butter

- 1 sprig rosemary

- 2 bay leaves

- 1 sweet onion (large; thinly sliced)

- 2 tablespoons sea salt

- 1 teaspoon whole peppercorn

Directions:

1. In a large skillet, heat the butter along with the pork belly until the cubes start to melt. Add the onion and sauté for approximately five minutes.

2. Remove the onions from the skillet and place it in the crock pot.

3. Next, add the rabbit pieces into the skillet and sauté on high heat until it becomes brown on all sides.

4. Add the wine to the skillet and allow it to evaporate for approximately 2-4 minutes. Pour all the contents from the skillet into the crock pot.

5. Add peppercorn, rosemary, bay leaves and salt to the crock pot. Cover and cook on low heat for 5-6 hours or until the rabbit becomes very tender.

Nutritional Information:

Calories: 517; Fat: 32 g; Protein: 36 g; Carbohydrates: 2 g

Balsamic Chicken

Serves: 6
Total Time: 4 hours 20 minutes
Equipment needed: A crock pot and a mixing bowl

Ingredients:

- 4 chicken breasts (boneless; halved)

- ½ cup balsamic vinegar

- 14.5 oz/400 g canned tomatoes (crushed)

- 1 onion (sliced)

- 4 garlic cloves

- 1 teaspoon rosemary (dried)

- ½ teaspoon thyme (dried)

- 1 teaspoon oregano (dried)

- 1 teaspoon basil (dried)

- 2 tablespoons olive oil (extra virgin)

- Salt and pepper (to taste)

Directions:

1. In a mixing bowl, season the chicken breasts with salt and pepper.

2. Coat the crock pot with the olive oil and place the chicken in it.

3. Place the garlic and onion slices on top.

4. Now add the dried basil, thyme, oregano and rosemary.

5. Finally add the vinegar and crushed tomatoes. Cook on high heat for approximately four hours or until the juices run clear.

6. Serve!

Nutritional Information:

Calories: 200; Fat: 6.8 g; Protein: 18.6 g; Carbohydrates: 17.6 g

Pork Chili Stew

Serves: 8
Total Time: 6 hours 20 minutes
Equipment needed: A crock pot and a skillet

Ingredients:

- 2 lbs/1 kg ground pork

- 8 slices of bacon (thick cut)

- 1 medium onion (yellow) (chopped)

- 3 small green peppers (chopped)

- 6 oz/170 g tomato paste

- 1 pack of chili seasoning

- 1 can of diced tomatoes (drained)

- 1 teaspoon garlic powder

- 1 teaspoon onion powder

- A dash of cayenne pepper

- Salt and pepper (to taste)

Directions:

1. Start by placing the onions and the pepper into the slow cooker.

2. In a skillet, cook the pork along with salt and pepper until it turns brown. Allow it to cool and add to the slow cooker.

3. Next, cut the bacon into small pieces and cook it the same way in your skillet. Allow it to cool and add to the slow cooker.

4. Drain the tomatoes and add that as well along with the tomato paste and the rest of the spices.

5. Cover and allow it to cook for approximately six hours on low heat.

Nutritional Information:

Calories: 492; Fat: 35 g; Protein: 31 g; Carbohydrates: 13 g

Cashew Chicken

Serves: 6
Total Time: 5 hours and 50 minutes
Equipment needed: a crock pot and a mixing bowl

Ingredients:

- 1½ lbs/750 g chicken thighs
- 1 bunch scallions (chopped)
- 1 lb/500 g cashews (raw)
- ½ onion (white; chopped)
- 3 tablespoons gluten-free fish sauce
- 2 tablespoons brown sugar
- 3 tablespoons gluten-free hoisin sauce (or soy sauce)
- 6 garlic cloves (minced)
- ¼ teaspoon white pepper
- Water

Directions:

1. Place the chicken in the crock pot.

2. In a mixing bowl, combine the scallions with fish sauce, hoisin sauce, garlic, sugar and pepper.

3. Pour the sugar mixture on top of the chicken along with the chopped onions.

4. Now add water to the crock pot so that the chicken is submerged in it completely.

5. Cook the chicken on high heat for approximately five hours.

6. Sprinkle the raw cashews on top and allow it to cook for another 30 minutes.

7. Serve!

Nutritional Information:

Calories: 651; Fat: 46.4 g; Protein: 30.6 g; Carbohydrates: 34.1 g

Conclusion

With a crock pot, preparing gluten-free meals becomes a whole lot faster and easier. You can enjoy the convenience of set and forget cooking with meals that are ready to be served when you are ready to eat. Slow cooked meals are also more nutritious and flavorful and with one dish, clean-up is fast and easy.

I hope this book was able to get you started with slow cooking and that you'll become as enthusiastic about the crock pot as I am!

Finally, if you enjoyed this book, please take a moment to leave a review on Amazon. Your feedback will help others learn how they can benefit from this book and also help me learn how I can better serve my readers. Thank you!

Other Books by Mike Moreland

If you would like to know more about gluten-free living and cooking, check out my other book in the *Gluten-Free Made Easy* series.

Gluten-Free Made Easy will make your transition to a gluten-free lifestyle as easy and effortless as possible. It contains everything you need to know to successfully jump-start your gluten-free diet today!

If you are thinking of going gluten-free but have no idea where to start or if you're already on a gluten-free diet but find it very hard to stick to, this book is for you. Also included in the book are 25 simple and delicious recipes for a gluten-free breakfast, lunch, dinner, dessert and snack.

Other Books by Mike Moreland

More Books

EFT Tapping: Quick and Simple Exercises to De-Stress, Re-Energize and Overcome Emotional Problems Using Emotional Freedom Technique

For an overview of my books see my author page: www.amazon.com/author/mikemoreland

Made in United States
Orlando, FL
16 December 2023